ACROSS THE MIDDLE

ENTREPRENEUR STRATEGIES FOR GROWTH AND SUCCESS

Marvin Carolina Jr.

ISBN-13: 978-0997878608
ISBN-10: 0997878606

Printed in the U.S.A.

Second Edition

CONTENTS

ACKNOWLEDGEMENTS

This book has been in the making for a long time. It started when I was selected to write articles for *The Kansas City Star* for leaders, entrepreneurs, and small-business owners in and around Kansas City. Due to my passion for those in the business community, it was evident in the articles, and knowing that I had business experience, as well as, a unique perspective, that my readers asked me to write a book; therefore, I did.

Guess what? I took my own advice! I worked closely with a team of phenomenal people and business professionals, and they helped me with this effort. Thank you for being an integral part of Team Carolina:

- Edward Long of Write It Right, for your research assistance and literary expertise (making sure my subject-verb agreement and spelling were correct).
- Dr. Amanda Goodson (Dr. G) of Amanda Goodson Global, for your support, wisdom and guidance through the process of publishing this book.
- Edward Cates of Nuance Marketing, for your creativity, marketing brilliance and designing an awesome book cover.
- Aunt Jane, thank you too! I was so excited when the manuscript arrived in the mail all marked up in red. Your feedback is priceless.

Without help from each of you, it would have taken me a *lot* longer to make this book a reality.

To the entrepreneur and small-business owner aspiring to grow their business, thank you for reading my book and for applying my strategies. Every word was written with you in mind.

To my lovely wife, Michelle, and my sons, Ellis & Ethan, who support me through it all. Thank you!

Dad, thanks for everything you and Mom did for me. You realized my potential and invested in it – for which I am grateful.

FOREWORD

There is no secret to becoming a successful business owner—you merely need to know what to do. Whether you already own your business or are considering starting a business, you owe it to yourself to read this book and get valuable advice from someone who has succeeded as a business owner.

Marvin Carolina Jr. has written an extraordinarily clear, easy to understand and insightful book that can literally change the way you live. He provides a comprehensive yet concise summary of the steps needed to make you a successful business owner. He explains what he learned on his journey and provides a complete view of each topic covered, using real-life scenarios to describe and provide context. Each chapter can be utilized independently, but the book was written to serve as a complete resource for anyone who is now, or is considering, becoming an entrepreneur or business owner.

As you accompany Marvin on this journey, continuously ask yourself these questions: "How can I apply this to my business?" "What am I doing that is working or not working?" "What changes do I need to make?" Your goal, after reading the book, should be to apply each principle covered. Each chapter is brief and easy to read because Marvin uses bite-size chunks of business-ownership wisdom.

As you read, ask yourself how you can apply what he is explaining, and start a consistent plan of action, which will lead you on your way to becoming a successful business owner.

Enjoy! Dr. Amanda Goodson

INTRODUCTION

You may have read that 80% of new businesses fail in their first eighteen (18) months or 90% of start-ups fail in their first five (5) years. These are alarming statistics, but fortunately, they are inaccurate. According to the U.S. Small Business Administration, nearly 70% of new businesses survive for at least two (2) years and about half of start-ups are still in business five (5) years later.[1]

Reality is rarely as bleak as rumors claim; and while I have no desire to scare you into reading my book, the truth is, there *is* a good chance your business will fail.

I have seen hundreds of businesses fail, so I know how a failed business can destroy a family, and a community. I have written this book to show you how to ensure your business not only survives, but thrives.

What makes this book different from others claiming to do the same thing? I know what you are going through. At one time, I was a business owner; therefore, I know the challenges you face, but not only do I know how to run a business, I know how to run a profitable business.

To realize your business' potential, you need three things:

- structure of a corporation
- innovativeness of an entrepreneur
- competitive fire of an athlete

I had all three and excelled as a business owner, so my perspective is unique because I competed—and excelled—in sports, business, *and* corporate America.

When I graduated from high school in Pittsburgh, I was an All-State football player. Graduating from Georgia Tech, I was a four-year football letterman.

My first job was at Oscar Mayer, in Sales, and I was promoted in less than a year. I was there five (5) more years, and confident that I knew everything I needed to know to succeed in business.

Eager to be my own boss, I launched Carolina Beverage Distributing, in Atlanta, in 1992. I was in business for six (6) years and did well—even though I was a sole proprietor, annual sales were nearly $1 million!

Returning to corporate America in 1998, working in Sears, Roebuck & Company's dealer stores, as Sales Manager, quickly being promoted to National Sales Manager. This took me to Chicago where I managed their Small Business Division for three (3) years.

In 2002, I accepted a job at JE Dunn Construction, one of America's largest construction-management companies, as a Director and was promoted to Vice President three (3) years later.

Upon arriving at JE Dunn, I knew how to run a successful business, and I quickly found a group in need of my experience and expertise. Minority construction contractors and women construction contractors in Kansas City, Missouri, were struggling to compete with their larger, established competitors, so I created a training program to help them.

The Minority Contractor Business Development (MCBD) Program, now in its eleventh year, teaches business-management skills by partnering participants with contractors and business professionals who serve as mentors.

The program was initially offered in Kansas City, but has been expanded, so it is now offered across the country: Atlanta, Austin, Charlotte, Dallas, Denver, Houston, Minneapolis, Nashville, Phoenix, Portland, and Savannah.

The program has been a resounding success: More than 80% of the program's graduates have increased their business sales, created jobs, *and* expanded their business capabilities. In addition, they have won more than 170 contracts with JE Dunn totaling more than $50 million!

The lessons I have shared for the last ten (10) years in the MCBD Program are the same lessons presented here, and the lessons presented here are identical to the lessons I began sharing in business articles in the *Kansas City Star*. This book, then, is simply a collection of some of those articles.

I have taught hundreds—if not thousands—of business owners how to run profitable businesses, so regardless of your industry, location, or the size of your business, these lessons will help.

*Entrepreneurship is like
playing football:
If you don't pay attention,
you'll get knocked out of
business.*

Chapter 1

Competition, Winning, and Talent

As a business owner, you need employees who are exceptionally good at what they do. You will make good hires if you analyze your applicants' attributes, skills, and talents.

- Attribute: An inherent characteristic (e.g., eye color).
- Skill: The ability to perform a task at a high level, which is performance that rates at least an 8 (eight) on a scale of 1 to 10, (ten being mastery). To have a skill, you must consistently perform a task at a high level and have an expert in that field, or an aptitude test, rate your performance as exceptional.
- Talent: A group of skills.

If you have all of the skills needed to do a job, then you have talent for that job; if you have the attributes and talent, you have the ability to excel at that job. I like using sports analogies, so consider the following.

National Football League (NFL) Quarterback

An NFL quarterback needs lots of attributes and skills. Here are a few: accuracy, attention-to-detail, competitiveness, composure, confidence, courage, focus, high threshold for pain, leadership, quick decision-making, pattern recognition, and resilience.

Not even the best quarterbacks have all of the attributes and skills, and while they lack in some areas, they excel in others. Some elite quarterbacks lack strong throwing arms, for example, but they make up for it by being exceptionally accurate.

Hiring a Quarterback

NFL executives go to great lengths to find collegiate quarterbacks who will become exceptional NFL quarterbacks, and business owners have to also go to great lengths to find exceptional employees. When vetting an applicant, do you examine their application or resume, verify education and experience, call their references, *and* conduct a background check?

Hiring a CPA

Assume you want to hire a certified public accountant (CPA). Like an NFL quarterback, a CPA needs lots of attributes and skills. Here are a few: ability to comprehend complex information; ability to work alone; analytical; attention-to-detail; bookkeeping; communication; conscientious, knowledge of laws, practices, and regulations; math; strategic thinking.

An exceptional CPA helps your business in several important ways:

Provides Advice: When business is going well and you are considering expanding, a CPA will tell you how much you should expand and how many new employees you will need. In short, they can help you make good financial and managerial decisions.

Conducts Audits and Saves Money: Your CPA will file your tax returns and related paperwork correctly and by the deadline, which will spare you from late filing fees. With their knowledge of ever-changing tax laws, they will take advantage of every allowance and benefit your business is eligible for.

Saves Time: With no more tax returns to file, you will be free to do what you do best: run your business.

Consequences

A bad quarterback can hurt his team; a bad CPA can *ruin* your business, and your life. Here are a couple of ways how:

Assume you hire an Ivy-League-educated Phi Beta Kappa who interviewed exceptionally well, had outstanding experience, excellent references, and had won an American Institute of Certified Public Accountants' Special Recognition Award. What could go wrong? If you give her too much control while providing too little oversight, *lots* could go wrong. An unethical CPA can tarnish your business's reputation—or ruin your business.

In one of America's biggest corporate scandals, a multi-billion-dollar, Houston-based, energy provider along with the accounting firm it had hired, engaged in accounting fraud. In 2000, the energy giant had revenues of $100 billion and its accounting firm had 85,000 employees. The energy giant is now bankrupt; the Chicago-based and former Big Five accounting firm, now has 200 employees, most of whom handle lawsuits against their company.[2]

Providing little or no accounting oversight can damage your reputation or ruin your business, but commonly-made accounting mistakes can also cause negative results in business. Assuming profit, always means positive cash-flow. Failing to communicate with your bookkeeper, failing to record small transactions, or not taking bookkeeping seriously enough, can have undesirable consequences.

Monitor and Evaluate

Once you have hired the best person for the job, you should monitor and evaluate their performance annually. A quarterback is evaluated by his team's coaches and owner, and a CPA is monitored by their state's Board of

Accountancy. Spend time and effort selecting the candidate who will do the job exceptionally well, and then evaluate them regularly. Study their application or resume, take detailed notes during their interview, call their references, and weigh their background check.

If monitoring and evaluating is done well, then your business will grow. If it is done poorly; however, then your business will go out of business.

If MONITORING and EVALUATING is done well, then your business will GROW.

Chapter 2

Find Talent and Build the Best Team

As a business owner you compete with rival businesses for the same customers and the same dollars. Some competitors are mom-and-pop shops and some are corporate behemoths. Are you doing all you can to win by fielding the best team possible? If you are not recruiting and retaining the best talent, you are not.

I have spoken to business owners across the country and have noticed a recurring theme: Business owners who produce high-quality products or provide high-quality services often complain about weak sales, yet they make little effort to find and hire talented workers.

I would like to define a few words here. You have *potential* if you occasionally perform a task exceptionally well and *skill* if you consistently perform a task exceptionally well. Talent, then, is simply a group of skills.

Here's an example:

Assume I want to be an accountant. If I can easily calculate long-division problems in my head and scored a perfect 800 in math on the SAT, do you think I have the talent to be an accountant? Though I am skilled at math in this example, I also need additional skills:

- Accounting Procedures and Regulations
- Analysis
- Attention to Detail
- Communication
- Critical Thinking
- Decision Making
- Judgment
- Negotiation
- Organization

If I demonstrate skill in all ten areas, I have the talent to become an exceptional accountant. However, if I have skill in only three or four areas, I almost certainly will not excel as an accountant.

How to Measure Talent
Talent may seem subjective, but it is not—you can measure it. More importantly, you should. Here are a few commonly-used indicators:

- Capabilities and Competencies (What can you do?)
- Experience (What have you done?)
- Intelligence (How smart are you?)
- Personality (How do you behave?)

Indicators alone cannot guarantee a new hire will excel, but conducting the analysis is better than not conducting it. Large companies have long used a battery of tools to screen prospective employees: applications, aptitude tests, background checks, drug tests, interviews, and references. Some even check your credit! Few business owners use all of these tools—most are content using two or three—and some do not use any of them, happy to hire a cousin or friend with no evidence this person can do the job.

Your business may be small, but that should not stop you from recruiting and retaining top-tier talent. Whether your goal is increasing market share or simply maintaining the share you have, you need to field the best team. So hire the best talent.

Your business may be small, but that should not stop you from recruiting and retaining TOP-TIER TALENT.

Chapter 3

You Need Rest to Be Your Best

Stop working nights and weekends.

It is easy to forgo sleep when you are running a business because you are doing everything—balancing the ledger, creating advertisements, making sales pitches, talking to customers—and you are also producing your product or providing your service.

With so much to do, you fall into bed around midnight and roll out of it at 6:00 a.m. You start each day the way you ended the previous one: tired and stressed. You get your morning coffee and after a cup, or several, you are ready for work. At least you think you are.

Caffeine keeps you alert—but only for a short time—by blocking sleep-inducing chemicals in your brain and releasing more adrenaline into your blood. According to researchers, if you drink no more than three eight-ounce cups of coffee per day, you face no health risks, but they also say caffeine is a poor substitute for sleep.[3]

Caffeine tricks your brain into thinking you do not need sleep when you actually do, and while it makes you more alert than you would be without it, you are not nearly as alert as you would be if you had gotten a good night's sleep.

A study concluded that adults who had gotten six (6) hours of sleep or less each night performed as poorly as the adults who had not slept for 48 hours![4] A study published in the Journal of Neuroscience found that staying awake too long kills brain cells in animals, and sleep researchers fear it has the same effect in humans.[5]

No matter how good you are at what you do, without adequate sleep, you will not perform at your best. If you have not gotten a good night's sleep, you may have some or all of these symptoms:

- Forgetfulness
- Impatience
- Inability to concentrate
- Inability to focus
- Inability to make good decisions
- Inability to solve problems
- Irritability
- Lack of creativity
- Lack of energy

A lack of sleep not only keeps you from performing at your best, it also causes health problems: diabetes, heart attacks, heart disease, heart failure, high blood pressure, and stroke.[6]

According to a Centers for Disease Control study, 35% of adults said they get less than seven (7) hours of sleep each night. Sleep experts recommend adults get seven (7) to nine (9) hours; some adults require more.[7]

Stop telling yourself you cannot afford to get seven (7) or eight (8) hours of sleep each night. You cannot afford not to! Whether your business is worth a few thousand dollars or a few million, you are its most-valuable asset. Take care of yourself, and stop working nights and weekends.

Whether your business is worth a few THOUSAND dollars or a few MILLION, you are its most-valuable ASSET.

Chapter 4

Why Would Anyone Start a Business?

According to the U.S. Small Business Administration, there are more small businesses in America than ever and more entrepreneurs and business owners than ever.[8] This is not surprising, but what *is* surprising is what a *US News and World Report* article revealed: "People who work for themselves are more likely than those who work for others to report that their jobs are stressful and exhausting and make them unhappy or depressed."

"Moreover, the typical American who works for himself or herself works 4.4 more hours per week than the typical person who is employed by someone else. And studies show that the typical entrepreneur earns less and has more variable income than the typical employee."[9]

Not the Same Thing

Entrepreneur and *business owner* are not synonymous. In fact, they have very different meanings.

In 1994, a thirty-year-old named Jeff Bezos became the youngest-ever vice president at the Wall Street investment bank D.E. Shaw & Company. Well-paid with a bright finance career ahead, Jeff had an idea. The World Wide Web was still relatively new, and he was sure there was a

Huge, untapped market for online commerce—he was so sure, he quit his job, moved to Seattle, and started Amazon, an online bookstore.

Amazon has performed well, so well that it has made Jeff the fourth-richest person in America.[10] He is an entrepreneur—not because he is rich—because he is an innovator. An entrepreneur puts a creative twist on a traditional business model. Jeff Bezos did not create bookstores, but he did create the first online bookstore.

A business owner, by comparison, operates a traditional business and tries to differentiate their business by providing a better product or service, a lower price, or a unique feature. Being a business owner may not seem glamorous, and it may not land you on the cover of *Forbes*, but it is no less important than being an entrepreneur.

Business owners create most of the new jobs in America, employ nearly half of the American workforce, and reflect our country's diversity. Businesses also introduce innovations, so while entrepreneurs may propel our economy forward, business owners are the very foundation of our economy. One is no better than the other; they are just different.

Why Do It?

If less money, longer hours, and more stress await the person wanting to open their own business, why are people flocking to self-employment? Job satisfaction. According to researchers, entrepreneurs and business owners derive more pleasure from work than people who work for someone else.[11] I have discussed this very thing with business owners across the country, and they have told me this is certainly true for them.

Job satisfaction explains why entrepreneurs and business owners continue working for themselves, but what makes a person open a business in the first place?

Some business owners have said if they had stayed at the companies they worked for, no matter how hard they would have worked nor how much they would have accomplished, they doubt they would have gotten the promotions they deserved.

Others have said they were tired of working jobs they were overqualified for, and the only reason they took them was to make ends meet until they found something better. Some started their own business because they were having trouble finding employment, so they created a business to create an income.

Others had worked in corporate America for decades and had amassed expertise and a long list of contacts, so they left the corporate world to do something on their own. Finally, some business owners refused to conform to the rules of corporate America. They went into business for themselves so they could wear jeans to work every day, set their own hours, and do things the way they wanted to do them.

Build a Solid Foundation

When traveling the country teaching business owners how to be successful, I am shocked at how many of them launched their businesses before they were ready—they thought they were ready but discovered, sooner or later, they were not.

Before they actually launched their business, they were selling their product or service and generating revenue, but there is lots more to be done.

No matter how small your business, it needs five (5) departments: accounting and finance, human resources, information technology, operations and marketing, and sales. You may sell the best product or service the world has ever seen, but if you devote 90% of your time producing it, you will not be in business long. You have to multi-task. Not only should you spend time in each department, you should also be good in each department.

Owning your own business is harder than it appears. I know from experience, and most business owners I have talked to say some version of this: "I had no idea it would be this difficult." In spite of the stress, uneven paydays, and long hours, if you lay a solid foundation, you will enjoy owning your own business.

In spite of the stress, uneven paydays, and long hours, if you lay a solid FOUNDATION, you will enjoy owning your own business.

Chapter 5

Do You Have the Skills to Succeed in Business?

To succeed in business, you need skills suited to your industry. No matter why you started your business, you should begin by taking inventory of your skills, so you know what you do well and what you do not do well. Select an industry you are ideally-suited for.

I like the Gallup Strengths Center's, Entrepreneurial Profile 10, because it identifies entrepreneurial talents, but whether you take this assessment or another one, it is important you find out what skills you have.

The most-successful business owners know what they are good at, and they enter industries ideally-suited for their skills. They also know what they are not good at, and they hire employees who are skilled in areas they (the business owners) are weak, which results in a business with few overlapping skills.

Your employees should have diverse skill sets, and it is obviously a bad idea for your accountant, advertising representative, human resources manager, and receptionist to have the same skills.

A business needs fifty skills to compete in the market. I have listed a few skill-pairs below. Which describe you?

- Generalist: Manages several parts of the business well
- Specialist: Manages only one part of the business well
- Doer: Prefers being hands-on in all areas of the business
- Manager: Prefers delegating but likes knowing what each area is doing
- Visionary: Able to envision new ways of doing things
- Detail-Oriented: Does things by the book
- Handler: Prefers working behind the scenes
- Seller: Enjoys communicating and persuading
- Planner: Enjoys formulating and following plans
- Spontaneous: Enjoys going with the flow

If you are a visionary, you continually think of ways to do things differently; but no matter how creative you are, your ideas do not become real without a detail-oriented planner. This is why your business needs employees with complementary skills.

It is perfectly fine for you to dabble in areas outside of your skill-set, but if you want to make your business as effective and efficient as possible, you will follow the example set by successful businessmen and businesswomen: Do what you do best and hire others to do the rest.

Do what you do BEST and HIRE others to do the rest.

Marvin Carolina Jr.

Chapter 6

Access to Capital

According to the U.S Small Business Administration, the primary reason small businesses fail to grow—especially women- and minority-owned small businesses—is lack of capital.[12] Small businesses rarely have access to external funds from public markets, and as a result, they are forced to rely on banks for capital.

A poll conducted by the Small Business Majority found that 90% of business owners said one of the biggest challenges they face is lack of access to sufficient capital and credit.[13] This is a problem. Without sufficient capital, you cannot grow your business.

I experienced this first-hand when I owned my business, so I know it is frustrating. Now that I teach business owners, what frustrates me are business owners who get capital, but have no idea how to spend it.

Before applying for capital, you should know how much you need. If you determine you need $57,000, for example, apply for that amount. Do not round-up and ask for $60,000. Only apply for the amount you need.

You should also know which form of capital is best-suited for your needs. In some cases, a line-of-credit makes more sense than a loan. Why? You would probably pay less interest with a line-of-credit because, unlike a loan, you would not get a lump sum.

You should also know what the money will be used for—be specific—and what impact that money will have on your business.

Assume you get a $100,000 loan, spend $10,000 of it, and leave the rest in the bank. You are earning 1% on the $90,000 in the bank, but you are paying 4% or 5% for the finance charge (on the borrowed amount). You did not need $100,000, and you would have been better off with a line-of-credit.

I cannot emphasize this enough: Capital or credit should propel your business forward! It is not wise to go into debt and be no better off. If you do not think a rational business owner would do this, think again. I am emphasizing this because I have seen rational business owners do this—I have even seen the same people do this again-and-again.

Do not use capital to dig yourself out of a financial hole because what usually happens is, you soon find yourself in another one. Why? Because you did not figure out why you were in the hole in the first place. Perhaps your estimate was wrong. You managed your project poorly.

Your workers were slow. Getting new capital only makes sense if you know why you need it.

I understand needing funds to move your business forward—I needed them for my business. However, experience taught me the cliché is true: You should not throw good money after bad. While it is tempting to seek capital when you see no other way out, using new money to pay for old mistakes will slowly but surely put you out of business.

*Using new MONEY to pay
for old MISTAKES will
slowly but surely put you
out of business.*

Chapter 7

How to Start a Business

(Part I)

Information-Gathering and Planning

More Americans than ever are leaving their employers and becoming their own bosses, and each year brings more business start-ups than the year before. Since so many people are starting businesses, it could not be that difficult to run a business, right?

Perhaps you have daydreamed about it, or perhaps you have actually been paid for your product or service. Either way, you are convinced you have what it takes to succeed as a business owner; you just need to know how to get started.

There are lots of things to consider before starting your business, but these are the most important things.

Why?

You need a business license to operate your business, and I suggest you write a business plan. Before taking action on either of these, though—or anything else—ask yourself this: Why do I want to own a business?

Running a business is extremely hard, and you will likely have more stress, make less money, and work longer hours than you would if you worked for someone else. I am not trying to dissuade you, but understand that running a business is difficult and requires enormous amounts of time and energy.

Being your own boss can be extraordinarily rewarding; however, but be sure you know why you have chosen to go into business for yourself.

What?

You have made your decision: You are starting your own business. The next question is, what will you sell? No matter what product or service you offer, you need to be an expert on it—you need to know everything about it.

I suggest you write at least thirty questions about your product or service, thinking of every conceivable question a prospective customer might ask, and then write the answers. Here are just a few of the many questions you should answer about your product or service:

- Am I offering it seasonally or year-round?
- Do I need insurance? If so, what kind?
- How fast can I produce or provide it?

- How is it different from similar products or services?
- How many can I produce in a week?
- How many customers can I service?
- How often will I offer it?
- How will I deliver it to my customers?
- What color is it?
- What size is it?
- Will I sell it repeatedly, or just once?

Who?

Once you have decided what you will sell, the next question is, Will there be a market for it? Just because your friend or cousin paid for your product or service does not mean there is a market for it. You need a sustainable market, which means people besides your friend or cousin are willing to buy what you produce.

Who will you sell to? Before answering, keep this in mind: Not everyone will need or want what you are offering. Customers choose you—not the other way around—so you have to identify who wants your product or service.

If you start a residential lawn-care service, for example, you will not advertise or market to corporations because they need a lawn-care provider with the equipment, expertise, and personnel to mow and maintain huge tracts of land. You have none of those things.

Where?

You have identified who you want as your customer, and now you have to find them and determine if there are enough of them to sustain your business. So you conduct a market survey.

The survey tells you if you have a viable customer base. A viable customer base is simply all the consumers in the market willing to buy your product or service—without a viable customer base, your business will not succeed.

You need to advertise and market to a large pool of prospective customers. For example, if your research determines your business can be profitable with one hundred customers, you have to find out how many prospective customers you need to advertise and market to in order to acquire those one hundred customers.

If you have to target twenty-five (25) prospective customers to acquire one customer, then you will have to advertise and market to 2,500 prospective customers to acquire 100 customers.

Once you determine what you will sell and who will buy it, you have to figure out how you will pay for producing it.

How?

When developing your budget, list every expense your business will have in the first twelve months—and be realistic. It does no good to underestimate expenses. A good business owner always looks for ways to reduce expenses, but when you are starting your business, ensure your budget includes everything you will need.

I will use the lawn-care service as an example. If you are deciding what equipment you will need to buy to get started and think borrowing shear cutters from one friend and a Weed Wacker from another friend is a good idea, think again.

You may save a few dollars borrowing items instead of buying them, but this is not a good business practice. Instead, decide what equipment you will need then go out and buy it.

If you are like most business owners, you will have lots of front-end capital; but you will spend it quickly and run out before the end of your first year. Later, when reflecting on your first year, you may regret some of the things you bought because you will realize that had you held on to more of your front-end capital, your business would be in a better financial position.

Be strategic. List the things you will need to launch your business and get it through the first year, and pay for those things up front.

I cannot emphasize this enough: Before going into business, think about every conceivable aspect of your business. What will you sell? Who will buy it? How much will it cost to provide it? Where will you get funding? Once you have answered all the necessary questions, you will have completed the information-gathering and planning phase.

How to Start a Business
(Part II)

Execution

You are certain you have an outstanding product or service, and people you have spoken to have convinced you your business will be successful. They have assured you they will be loyal customers, and since you are eager to submit your two-week notice and become your own boss, you are sure now is the time to start your business.

You have determined how much capital you need for the first year, but be prepared to tap into your savings or 401K before you get any business—the vast majority of business owners I know had to. If you spend too much on front-end expenses, you may not be able to afford to do your first piece of business. In addition, since you have no customers, you have no income.

If you hire employees, but have no work for them to do, you are paying them to do nothing. I know business owners who started this way—business owners who are intelligent and accomplished in their fields—but they were so eager to get started, they failed to plan.

You have created your budget, so you can begin buying what you need, but spend wisely. Businesses fail for lots of reasons, but one of the most-common reasons is business owners spend more than they should up-front. Why?

They buy things they think they need, but later discover they did not need them after all. If you buy things you do not need, or do not need at the outset, when you get your first contract and need money to fulfill the order, you may not have the funds.

Similarly, if your business needs employees, do not hire all of them at once. This example shows why.

Assume you are opening a pizza shop with delivery service and have determined you need five (5) delivery drivers. If you hire all five (5) of them at once, you may only have enough deliveries to keep them busy half of the day.

Perhaps less, so you will be paying them to sit around most of the day.

Your pizza shop may eventually need five drivers, but in the first month or two, you may only need one or two drivers; therefore, only hire one or two. No matter what kind of business you have, hire employees incrementally so you are not wasting money by paying employees who have nothing to do.

How to Start a Business
(Part III)

Growing

After being in business for a year or two, two things become apparent: You have what it takes to run a successful business, and there is a market for your product or service. The next step is growing your business—every year.

There are two components to business growth: efficiency and sales.

Not So Fast

Your goal is to grow your business each year, but resist the temptation to grow too fast. Adding customers you cannot service in a timely manner is bad business. Strive for incremental growth by determining how many customers your business can comfortably add each year based on your business's capacity. If your employees are operating efficiently, but are not at their capacity, you then have the capacity to add customers.

If you want to add customers, but can only do so by hiring more employees, only add as many employees as you are certain you can pay—while remaining profitable. Hiring lots of employees to win a contract may be tempting, but a closer examination of your numbers may reveal hiring these new employees will actually reduce profits.

New Business

When you have hit your yearly profit margins and are planning for the upcoming year, strive to increase your volume by at least 10%; but ensure your new business is at least as profitable as your existing business. Ideally, you will be able to scale, meaning adding customers, without adding overhead. The more you scale, the more profitable your business will be.

Efficiency

Efficiency is doing things quickly and correctly to produce the desired result. The only way to realize your business's potential is by ensuring it operates at peak efficiency, which it will do if your employees are working at optimal levels. Continually look for tasks and processes that are inefficient, and improve them or get rid of them.

Sales

No matter how great your product or service, you have to sell it; and sales, more than any one thing, contributes most to business growth. In the hundreds of training sessions I have conducted with business owners across the country, when a business has underperformed, it is usually because its owner and employees are not spending enough time selling their product or service. How much time should you spend?

If your business is new, you and your employees should spend at least 80% of your time selling; after a couple of years, you can spend as little as 30% of your time selling. I am not suggesting other areas of your business are not important, but to grow your business, you and your employees have to continue servicing your existing customers while adding new customers.

Great companies are great at sales. Herbalife, for example, offers an excellent product, but lots of struggling companies also offer great products. What makes Herbalife great is, they are committed to outselling the competition—they go out and ask people for their business.

Your business should revolve around sales. Every day. As Thomas Watson, IBM's founder, once said, "Nothing happens until somebody sells something."

---

*Your business should
revolve around SALES.
Every day.*

Chapter 8

Profit

If you are like most business owners, you went into business to make money. Nothing wrong with that. I have found, though, there are lots of business owners who want to make money, but simply do not know how.

Revenue

Revenue is income received from making a sale, and while it indicates how much business you are doing, take it with a grain of salt. Revenue does not include fixed and variable costs, so it does not convey how efficiently your business is run.

Do not obsess over revenue. It *is* important, and you should continually look for ways to increase it; but if your goal is to make money, your primary concern should not be increasing revenue.

Profit

If you only remember one thing I have said to this point, make it this: Focus more on profit and less on revenue.

Profit and revenue, though used interchangeably, mean very different things. *Revenue* is what you make from a sale; *profit* is what you keep. Profit, also known as *earnings*, is what remains after you have paid all your fixed and variable costs. You decide what you will do with your profit (e.g., buy equipment, hire employees, pay yourself).

If you want your business to grow you have to find ways to increase profit—not revenue. Profit does not automatically increase simply because revenue has increased. How? It happens when you fail to control costs.

Assume you won a contract for a $100,000 job, but to complete the job, you have to hire staff, rent or buy additional equipment, and require your employees to work around-the-clock to meet the deadline. This $100,000 job may cost you $100,000 to complete!

In construction we call a job like this, a job with little-to-no profit, a *junk job*. To assure you do not waste your time on a junk job, do not become engrossed with revenue; analyze the numbers.

Profit Margin

It is ironic that of the three terms—*revenue, profit, and profit margin*—revenue and profit are the most-often discussed, but profit margin is the most important and least understood.

Profit is sales minus costs, and *profit margin* is profit divided by sales. Profit margin is expressed as a percentage and is the best indication of how efficiently your business is run. Routinely compare your business's profit margin to your competitors' profit margins to see how well you are controlling costs.

Comparing profit margins for jobs can also help you select the best job. Of the jobs below, which would you choose?

- $1,000,000 in revenue with 5% profit margin
- $800,000 in revenue with 10% profit margin
- $600,000 in revenue with 15% profit margin

It bears repeating: Do not obsess over revenue. Most business owners I know talk primarily about revenue, and when I owned my business, I obsessed over revenue. If I had been given these scenarios when I was in business, I would have jumped at the chance to make $1,000,000, but I eventually learned it is important to dig deeper and analyze the numbers.

Why Run Slower?

I began running several times per week and several miles each time, to lose weight, and I assumed if I ran faster, I would burn more calories. My conditioning improved dramatically, which is not surprising, but I was disappointed: According to my scale, I had only lost a couple of pounds!

I was in excellent shape—good enough shape to run a half-marathon—but my goal was to lose weight. Not get in shape.

I began wearing a Fitbit, a fitness activity band that measures heart rate and calories burned, and was shocked when it said I was running too fast for optimal weight loss. Since my goal was to burn fat and lose weight, I should have actually been running slower.

Bigger Jobs for Less Money?

Several construction contractors have told me business is so good, they are considering bidding for bigger jobs. I have a problem with this. Each of them have healthy profit margins, which will almost-certainly shrink if they accept bigger jobs. The bigger jobs will bring more revenue, but they will also bring more costs—most importantly, they will bring fewer profits.

Bigger jobs will bring more REVENUE, but they will also bring more COSTS—most importantly, they will bring fewer PROFITS.

Marvin Carolina Jr.

Chapter 9

Embrace Technology

You have the saying, "If it ain't broke, don't fix it." It sounds like ancient wisdom, but it is not: T. Bert Lance, a government employee, is credited with popularizing this expression in 1977. As a business owner, to stay ahead of the competition—or even keep pace with it—you must find ways to operate more effectively and efficiently. Technology helps you do both.

Brian Moran, a small business expert, said technology has made it possible for small businesses to compete with large businesses. The problem is, small businesses are not fully using it. According to Brian, "Business owners are not embracing *all* of the existing technology at their disposal. According to several different studies, small businesses are only using about 30% to 35% of their existing technology's capabilities. Imagine what they can do if they were using 75% of their technology's capabilities?"[14]

Technology makes your business more efficient. Most business owners I have talked to have no problem buying and using the latest gadgets and software—they do not know how the gadgets and software will actually help their business.

Assume you only have one competitor, and the two of you employ office managers with identical salaries. Your office manager dabbles in technology, so your business operates at 30% of its technological capability; your competitor's office manager is a technology wiz, so their business operates at 90% of its technological capability.

In this scenario your competitor's business is three times more efficient than yours, and their employees are three times more efficient than yours. Here is some perspective: Your competitor's office manager will have done as much work by 3:00 p.m. on Tuesday of every week as your office manager will do the entire week.

A 2013 survey of business owners found that while 51% of them use technology for accounting, they use it less often for other things—scheduling appointments (39%), managing customer relations (34%), point-of-sales (25%)—but what shocked me was, less than half of them (48%) have a website![15]

You *have* to have a website. It allows customers and prospective customers to get information about your product or service, day or night. It helps you reach more people than you would have reached had you used a traditional advertising campaign, and conveys your business will be around for a long time. If your website is set-up to allow it, customers and prospective customers can also make purchases.

A well-designed and well-written website also creates a good first impression by implying your business is well-run and your product or service is outstanding.

More than half of all business owners are losing money because they do not have a website. According to California-based Merrill Research, "If you take your online presence seriously, there is no better way to compete" with larger competitors.[16]

Even if you have a website, laptop, and smartphone and are already using accounting software, by adding a few things, your business will run much better—and you will make more money.

There are lots of gadgets and software packages to choose from, but only buy what your business needs. Here are a few software items that will make your business more efficient. Each software has several brands, so choose the one that best suits your needs:

- Batchbook: Provides demographic information about customers and prospective customers.
- Evernote: Organizes appointments and business meetings, which you can access from your computer, smart phone, or tablet.
- Google Analytics: Tracks how many people visit your website and which web pages they view.
- MailChimp: Creates newsletters and e-mails them to your contacts.

- PHP Point-of-Sale: Allows customers to buy products or services on your website.
- QuickBooks: Maintains your accounting.
- Skype: Allows you to meet without leaving your office.
- WordPress: Creates and maintains your blog.

Since you are the owner, you do not have to run your business *and* wear the technology hat. Hire someone to wear it. Be sure they know what they are doing, then have them install the software throughout the business.

Today's business environment is not the same as it was previously, so do not cling to what previously worked. Before, if someone called while you were on the phone, they got a busy signal; now they get voicemail. You once made accounting entries with an accounting sheet, a pencil, and a calculator; now you should use accounting software.

Technology makes your business and your employees more efficient and gives your business a competitive advantage. The opposite is also true. So whether you want the largest share of the market or simply want to maintain the share you have, your business has to be efficient.

TECHNOLOGY makes your business and your employees more EFFICIENT and gives your business a competitive ADVANTAGE.

Chapter 10

Which Guides Your Business:
Map or GPS?

I was explaining to a friend, who is also a business owner, that if he wants to grow his business, he has to use state-of-the-art technology and best practices. He told me he had driven his daughter to college, and he had used printed directions from MapQuest. So I said, "Welcome to 2015—people don't use maps anymore. They use GPS."

What is the Difference?

It is never a good idea to take your eyes off the road when driving, but if you are using a map or written directions, you occasionally have to. MapQuest is an improvement over a printed roadmap because it provides directions, but this is not much of an improvement because you have to take your eyes off the road to read them.

With GPS, you keep your eyes where they should be—on the road—and the voice tells you where you will turn and how much farther before you turn. GPS also offers lots of helpful information: fastest route, gas stations, lodging, places to eat, rest stops, and traffic conditions.

Business GPS

GPS stands for "Global Positioning System," but I use it to mean "Guide to Profit and Success." If GPS guides your business, you are using cutting-edge technology and best practices, which were designed to help you run your business more effectively and efficiently and make your life easier.

Why would you not use them? If your response is, "What I've done has always worked," then I say this: By using the latest streamlined processes, your competitors are getting more done than you—in less time and at a lower cost.

It previously took two days to take inventory, because you had to count every item on your shelves or in your warehouse. Now, you should not take inventory this way, because electronic cash registers do the same thing instantly.

Too Expensive?

Since the market is saturated with technology, their prices have dropped; and what was once expensive is now affordable. Here is just one example.

When Garmin introduced its Street Pilot 2720 in 2005, which was one of the industry's first GPS', it was more than $1,000. In 2015 Garmin's top-of-the-line model sold for $400, and its least-expensive model sold for $129.

Even at the lowest price, its 2015 model was more sophisticated than its 2005 model.

Cutting-edge technology is available for you to use, so are best practices. In today's global market where everyone is trying to get an advantage, you cannot afford to not use them.

Trim the Fat

Assume you decide to market your product or service primarily on social media, and you want to reach as many non-business people as possible. What would you say if your marketing director suggested marketing on Myspace?

Myspace has 50 million worldwide users; Facebook has 1.49 *billion*. Marketing on Myspace was a good idea years ago, but not anymore. Take a look around your business—what relics are you preserving?

If you are not using cutting-edge technology and best practices, I can guarantee two things are true: Your business is grossly inefficient, and it is losing market share.

I meet weekly with business owners across the country, and I am happy to discover more-and-more of them are modernizing their businesses. Smart business owners know they have no choice because customers continually demand lower prices, which only the leanest and most-efficient businesses can provide.

SMART business owners know they have no choice because customers continually DEMAND lower prices, which only the leanest and most-efficient businesses can provide.

Chapter 11

What Does the Data Say?

When I ask "How's business?" what I really want to know is, how well do you know your business? The response I often get is, "Sales are up." That may be a good thing, but it is not necessarily—if you are tracking your data, you will know if it is or not.

What is Data?

Data is simply numbers and information you should track. Here are a few numbers you should track daily:

- Gross profit
- Net profit
- Profit margin
- Revenue
- Sales

Here is some information you should track daily:

- Customer surveys
- What your competitors are doing
- Where your customers live
- Which product or service sells best and why

In addition, look for technology that will make your business more efficient—and more profitable.

Where Are the Numbers?

You will find these numbers in your balance sheet, which show assets, liabilities, and equity. As the name implies, your balance sheet *must* balance. You should also be familiar with your income statement (or profit-and-loss statement), which shows revenue and expenses for a given period (e.g., year-to-date) from operating and non-operating activities.

Tracking these numbers will tell you the source of every dollar you make, and it will also tell you where every dollar goes. Surprisingly, not every business owner tracks their numbers, so doing so will give you a competitive advantage.

Not Just the Numbers

You should also track information, and the more customer demographic information you track—age, education, ethnicity, gender, geographic location, income, marital status, race—the more specific your customer becomes. This is important: You have to know who your customer is.

Assume you are a real-estate agent, and 65% of your business comes from 40 to 55 year-olds. Does it make good business sense, in your effort to attract new clients, to spend all of your resources advertising and marketing in a magazine whose target audience is 20 year-olds?

While this *is* a good age group to attract—and you can spend some time trying to attract them—your data says you should allocate at least 65% of your resources advertising and marketing to 40 to 55 year-olds.

Where are Your Customers?

Find your customers, go to them. Advertise where they are, meet them where they are, and socialize where they are. By relying on your data, you will spend your time and resources connecting with your customers in the most effective and efficient manner.

If your business is in Kansas City, Missouri, but 70% of your clients live in Lee's Summit, Missouri, then you should follow your data and spend at least 70% of your time canvassing for clients in Lee's Summit.

Equipment

Tracking numbers and customer information is important, but you should also track inventory and equipment. Assume you own a delivery service with four trucks. One of the first things you need to know is, how much money does each truck make? To answer, you have to know how much it costs to maintain each truck. Here are those costs:

- Fuel
- Insurance
- Labor
- Maintenance
- Miscellaneous expenses (e.g., tires)
- Tax (e.g., business, property)

It is important that you know how much revenue and profit each truck is capable of earning. If your trucks are operating at 50% capacity and business increases requiring more deliveries to be made, do not rush out and buy a truck; increase the workload on the trucks you already have.

Does This *Really* Help?

Perhaps your business is fine, you have lots of clients, and you are making money. While that is great, do not forget your competitors want your clients; and they are always looking for ways to make your customers their customers.

Do not become complacent and assume what has always worked will continue to. It will not. Get to know your business—really know it—study your data, and base your decisions on that data.

Do not become COMPLACENT and assume what has always worked will continue to.

Chapter 12

What You Avoid Can Put You Out of Business

When I owned my business in Atlanta, I was surprised at how well my business was doing. While I was making lots of money, I could not understand why I was not able to keep much of it. I told myself having high revenue, but low profit was probably normal in business and assured myself if I kept making lots of sales, profit would increase.

Looking back, I realize I should have followed my instincts and talked to someone, instead of putting it off.

What I eventually learned was, high revenue with low profit indicated my costs were too high; and in order for my business to survive, I had to slash costs. It sounds simply now, but I had no idea then. If I had taken time to talk with someone, they surely would have told me this. I learned a lesson, but not in time to save my business.

As a business owner, you have lots to do just to keep your business running. When trying to incorporate changes to make your business run more effectively and efficiently, your heavy workload only gets heavier. It is easy to put-off things that are not part of your routine because your routine keeps you busy enough. After all: Where will you find time?

Not So Bad

Tim Pychyl, a researcher at Carleton University in Ottawa, Canada, who wrote *Solving The Procrastination Puzzle*, said when you put pressure on yourself to accomplish a task, you develop a "strong reaction to the task at hand, and so the story of procrastination begins there with what psychologists call task [aversion]."[17] In other words, the more you do not want to do something, the more you will avoid doing it.

Consider the tasks you are avoiding—are you telling yourself you *have* to complete them? That you really do not want to complete them? If so, stop. According to Mr. Pychyl, when you tell yourself this, you will put-off completing these tasks.

Here are three things you can do to get things done:

1. Organize

Put the tasks that are not urgent in a separate pile, and come back to them when you have time. When you come back, arrange the non-urgent tasks in chronological order and estimate how much time you expect to spend on each of them.

It is not necessary to begin with the most-important task, so begin with the task that will take the least amount of time. The most important task may be the most difficult and most time-consuming—if putting it off will not jeopardize your business, put it off.

2. Jump In

People tend to overestimate how much motivation they need to do something, so they look at a task and doubt they will have the desire or energy to complete it. Or they think they will start and get stuck. Just start! Once you start and begin making progress, gaining confidence and momentum, you will want to continue.

This is another reason you should start with the task that will require the least amount of time: It will require relatively little time and effort. Some call this picking low-hanging fruit, which is a metaphor for doing the easiest thing first.

3. Reward Yourself

Psychological studies have shown that using rewards is an excellent form of motivation, so use them for yourself and your employees. You may spend lots-and-lots of hours on your business while allowing yourself little time for relaxation. Reward yourself with dinner and a movie—or whatever you enjoy.

Easy Does It

Today's business climate, which says you are not working if you are not working on several tasks at once, requires you to multi-task. When you are working on tasks you have been putting off, work on one-at-a-time, because if you try to do too much too quickly, you might overwhelm yourself; and fail to complete any of the tasks.

Gets Easier

You may be surprised to find that after you have completed the first task you had been putting off, you are eager to begin working on the second. While I am no scientist, I remember Newton's First Law, which says an object at rest stays at rest and an object in motion stays in motion.

This law is not limited to objects. When you address whatever you have been putting off, it will get easier. So stop procrastinating and making excuses.

When you ADDRESS whatever you have been putting off, it will get EASIER.

Chapter 13

Is Inefficiency Stealing from Your Business?

Efficiency and effectiveness are not the same thing. *Efficiency* is doing something quickly and correctly, and *effectiveness* is doing the right things.

Inefficiency hurts your business in several ways: It increases costs, forces you to spend more money than you should and wastes time. Each of these reduces profit and makes your business less competitive.

Assume you are awarded a $100,000 contract, but the materials needed for the job arrive late. Your workers arrive at 8:00 a.m. each day, but with no materials to work with, they sit around and wait. This wasted time costs you $10,000; so your profit margin—which was 15%—has fallen to 5%.

Inefficiency is often hard to find, so when searching your business for it, do not overlook a single department, practice, or procedure. Here are several ways to increase efficiency:

Audit

Routinely audit your business. Replace ineffective practices that no longer do what you originally intended, and revise inefficient procedures that erode your bottom-line. And get employee feedback. Your employees probably know better than you what works and what does not. Ask for their input, and trust their expertise.

Document

Keep a record of your practices, procedures, and processes; make them available to your employees; and make sure your employees can easily find them. By doing so, both veteran employees and new hires can quickly find answers to procedural questions.

Evaluate

Routinely review your supplier relationships, considering things like rate of on-time delivery and customer service. If you find you are frequently waiting for a supplier to return your calls when you have a problem, for example, consider finding a new supplier.

Maintain

Most business owners do not provide routine maintenance on their office equipment, but when their equipment breaks down, they wish they had. Maintenance is not a luxury expense, so do not put it off. It is more cost-effective to perform routine maintenance rather than wait until you are forced to replace a piece of equipment.

Outsource

If there is an area your business lacks expertise, or if it takes too much time performing a task, consider outsourcing. You can easily find service professionals who will handle your bookkeeping, marketing, or human resources tasks, for example; and not only will they save you time, they will do a better job than you would have done.

Train

If your employees lack cutting-edge skills, your business will lose any competitive advantage it has. Ensure your employees are routinely learning new skills and keeping abreast of industry changes. In addition, cross train your employees; so in the event of illness or vacation leave, your business will continue to run smoothly.

Upgrade

It is often cost-effective to replace humans with machines. For example, instead of having employees carry gravel back-and-forth, it may be better to buy a conveyor belt to do the work. The conveyor belt would require a larger one-time cost, but with proper maintenance, it will carry the gravel more efficiently than your employees —and the conveyor will not call- in sick or ask about your benefit package.

Inefficiency is everywhere. If your employees are arriving at work late or leaving early, they are inefficient. If your delivery trucks take longer routes than necessary, they are inefficient. Look at everyone and everything, and weed-out these costly culprits.

Look at everyone and everything, and weed-out these costly culprits.

Marvin Carolina Jr.

Chapter 14
What is Your Business Worth?

When sales are strong and your business is doing well, you may not think much about retirement; when you do, you may tell yourself that when you are ready to sell your business, you will get a good price and live comfortably off the proceeds. What if you cannot get a good price for your business? Or worse—what if no one wants to buy your business!

American Express surveyed business owners, and 60% of them said they are not on track to save the money needed for retirement; 73% said they are worried they may not save enough to have the lifestyle they want when they retire.[18]

If you have no plans for selling your business, you will need to replace the income you receive from your business with another income stream; or, you may be planning to sell, but not at this time. Whether you plan to sell in the near-future or the distant-future—or not at all—run your business as if you intend to sell it. To do so, you have to know what it is worth.

When determining your business's value, overlook sentimental value. Sentimental value is not actual material worth: It is value that comes from a personal or emotional attachment.

You may have spent years working ten-hour days, and your business may have helped you put your kids through college; but the market does not care. Sentimental value adds zero market value. A prospective buyer or investor wants to know one thing: How much can they make from your business? This is their only concern, and it should be your only concern.

Whatever gives your business a competitive advantage increases your business' value. Here are five ways to do that:

Contracts

What kinds of contracts do you have (one-year, three-year, ten-year)? You obviously need profitable books, but contracts add value by guaranteeing future revenue. There are several advantages of using multi-year contracts:

- lowers costs
- provides continuity of production while avoiding annual start-up and phase-out costs
- provides incentives for contractors to improve productivity
- reduces administrative burdens
- stabilizes contractor plans and workforces

Patents

If you have a patented process, your competitors cannot duplicate it. Here are additional advantages:

- encourages settlement in litigation disputes
- expands market share because your product can be licensed in other geographical locations
- higher profit margins because you can charge higher prices for your patented product
- prevents theft
- reduces competition because of entry barriers for competitors

Equipment

If you have state-of-the-art equipment, a buyer would not need to upgrade.

Name Recognition

Having a recognizable business with a good reputation adds tremendous value; but your business has to have a good reputation from the consumer's perspective. *You* may think your business is the best in the industry, but what counts is what consumers think.

Brand and name recognition connects your business to potential customers, and once they become customers, it keeps them coming back.[3]

Workforce

If your workforce is experienced and works well together, a buyer would not need to find and hire employees.

Your business and your home are probably your two biggest investments, so get in the habit of increasing the value of each of them. When I was younger, I loved shag carpet—I thought it was cool. It was cool in the '70s but not anymore, which is why I ripped it out and installed new carpet. I *still* love shag carpet; the market, however, does not.

There are several ways to determine your business' value, but remember: What matters is what it is worth to someone else, not to you.

If you need an official, professionally-prepared business valuation, you will spend at least $3,000 —and a lot more if you need a detailed valuation and your business is unusually complex.

An official business valuation requires three weeks of probing your business' finances, management structure, and operational structure. If you do not need an official valuation, you can calculate the value yourself using one of the approaches below:

Asset-Based

How much will it cost to replace your assets with equipment in similar condition? If the value of your business assets are greater than your earnings, use this approach.

Market

Determine your business' value by comparing it to comparable businesses (i.e., businesses with similar assets) in the market. Do not use this approach; however, if your business operates differently from comparable businesses.

Income

Determine value by looking at earnings. This approach determines business value based on its income-producing capacity and risk:

- Determine future earnings: Look at the last three years' earnings, and calculate your three-year average.
- Determine your multiple: If your average earnings are $100,000 or less, use a multiple of two. If between $100,000 and $500,000, use three. If average earnings are more than $500,000, use four.
- Add your net liquid assets: What will your business have left after all its debt—bonds, cash, equipment, real estate, stock—is paid? Add the total value of your net liquid assets to your average earnings (from previous step).

Most businesses sell for two- to three-times the amount of their earnings.

If you do not need an official valuation, but are not good at math, there is another option: You can buy an online valuation. BizEquity, one of several online business-valuation services, charges about $365 for a twenty-three-page report.

Whether you pay for a business valuation or calculate it yourself, find-out what your business is worth. In addition, continually upgrade your equipment, processes, technology, and workforce so when you are ready to sell, someone other than you will see the value in your business.

Whether you pay for a business valuation or calculate it yourself, find-out what your business is worth.

Chapter 15

Not Too Fast

When I previously watched long-distance races on television, I wondered why runners let other runners pass them and get a big lead. I continued to wonder why until I began running half-marathons. What I discovered was, some runners I tried keeping pace with were in better shape than me.

I kept pace with them for two or three miles, then I would fade, and runners who had been behind me, running at their pace, would pass me. I quickly learned to not concern myself with keeping pace with other runners—I had to focus on running as fast as I comfortably could.

Set Your Own Pace

What does running have to do with running a business? Plenty. Regardless of which you are running, you perform best when you are at a comfortable pace; and only you know what pace is comfortable.

Some will say you are too slow and that if you work faster, you will sell more products or services and make more money. They *are* right, but there is a danger in moving too fast. I have observed hundreds of business owners, and when a business owner speeds-up and works faster than they are comfortable with working, they usually lose control of their business.

Be Comfortable

Going at your pace not only means working at a speed you are comfortable with—it also means performing tasks you are comfortable performing. Here is an example of a not-so-obvious way of moving too fast:

Assume a salesperson tries convincing you your business needs new accounting software, and they tell you all of your competitors use it. You are accustomed to doing your accounting by hand, and you are usually accurate; but the salesperson assures you, you will have no more accounting errors, and it will require less time and effort to do your accounting.

You buy and install the software before realizing a not-so-small problem: You have no idea how to use it. You may try to figure it out, spending more time than you originally did and making more mistakes than before, or you may not use it at all.

Speed *Is* Important

When I say do not move too fast, do not assume I am saying take your time—I am not. When you move slower than your competitors, you *will* miss opportunities because your competitors will get to prospective customers before you. Business success is not completely reliant on speed, but speed is a factor.

When pursuing a prospective customer, if a competitor arrives first, they will get first consideration. No matter how good your product or service—even if it is the industry's best—though the prospective customer may like what you are selling, it will not matter if they have already signed a contract with your competitor.

If you begin hearing "Had you been here a week earlier …," this indicates you should quicken your pace. When I talk about pace, I am reminded of Mr. Tudball, the slow-moving character Tim Conway played on *The Carol Burnett Show*. In business, you should not move too fast, but do not shuffle along like Mr. Tudball either.

In my training class, I noticed, some business owners were working faster and some slower. What was funny was, some of the slower-moving owners wondered why their faster-moving peers were having better luck.

It was apparent to me, that their faster-moving peers were completing ten steps in two days while they were completing the same ten steps in two weeks—so they should not expect the same results! Also, while some of their real-world competitors will move faster, what is most important is, them moving as fast as their comfort level.

Having Too Much

Some business owners fail because they lack something they need. Some because they either have something they do not know how to use, and others because they have something. they should not have.

Assume you own a restaurant that serves excellent food. Your friend says, since so many of your customers come from the south side of town, you should open a second restaurant there. Seems like a good idea.

Expanding too soon is a common problem in the restaurant industry. This may seem like a good idea in this scenario, but before expanding, you should ensure your management structure is in place and that you have permanent staff at your initial location.

Similarly, someone may tell you that if you have been in business a certain number of months, you should have a certain number of customers. The person who says this has probably not considered that if you had that number of customers, you might drown from too much business. Someone may try to convince you, you should hire ten or fifteen employees, not knowing you can only manage four or five.

When competitors are ahead of you in business—even way ahead—do not try catching them, if it means working faster than you are accustomed to working. Find and maintain your pace, and whether you overtake the others or not, you *will* finish the race.

*Find and maintain your
pace, and whether you
overtake the others or
not, you will finish the
race.*

Chapter 16

Are You Informed?

Some things are more important than others. As a business owner, knowing whether you can afford to hire the talented applicant with impressive credentials is more important than knowing the unemployment rate. Similarly, knowing if your wedding cakes will arrive at your client's wedding on time is more important than knowing the price of a barrel of oil.

Economic indicators you hear on the news may not seem to affect your business, but if you look closely, you will see they do.

The unemployment rate indicates whether there are too many people looking for work or too few. If too many, the unemployment rate is high; so you can offer that talented job applicant less money because you have lots more applicants to choose from. If too few, the unemployment rate is low; and since there fewer applicants, you will have to offer more.

Get It Somewhere

It is important you stay abreast of economic news, emerging products and trends in your industry, and changes in government regulations. By doing so, you will know about opportunities for growth, changes in the market, or threats to your business. You can also get in-depth information and analysis by reading trade publications and blogs written by industry experts.

Few business owners, I have discussed this with, said they read industry-specific articles, so if you do, you give yourself a competitive advantage.

Get the Word Out

Companies are looking for environmentally-friendly ways to do business—and for good reason. Studies show companies using environmentally-friendly products and processes tend to have healthier workplaces. Often times, qualifying for environmental tax breaks, and produce less waste.

While each of these are important, the primary reason most executives and business owners use green technology is, it helps them make more money.

If your business is going green, let the public know. Put it in your marketing. More consumers than ever are buying products and services from companies whose values align with their own. These consumers will look favorably on your recycling program or your environmentally-friendly manufacturing processes.

How is the Economy?

The American economy is enormous, and there are lots of economic indicators that provide insight on how segments of it are performing. The Dow Jones Industrial Average is the most popular indicator, and while it *is* important, the following indicators tend to have more impact on small businesses than the Dow:

Consumer Confidence Index (CCI): Measures consumer opinion about the economy. An increase indicates consumers have confidence in the economy and in their own financial health, so they are more likely to spend. A decrease indicates they are less likely to spend and more likely to save. An upward-trending CCI suggests business owners increase output, and a downward-trending CCI suggests business owners decrease output.

Consumer Price Index (CPI): Measures the change in price for a group of goods and services. CPI is the most-accurate indicator of inflation, and it hints which direction interest rates will likely go. An increase in CPI is usually followed by an increase in interest rates, while a decrease in CPI is usually followed by a decrease in interest rates.

Gross Domestic Product (GDP): Measures the market value of goods and services. GDP is important because it gives an idea of what is ahead. A stronger-than-expected increase in GDP means prices will likely rise, and a weaker-than-expected increase means prices will likely fall. A weak GDP indicates an economic slowdown, and to remedy this, the government often lowers interest rates in hopes of stimulating the economy.

Producer Price Index (PPI): Measures how much producers are paying for goods and raw materials. PPI and CPI are linked. When PPI rises, business owners tend to raise prices to offset their higher costs. A word of caution: If the economy is in an economic slowdown, as a business owner, think twice about raising prices because consumers will be looking for lower prices. If you are forced to raise prices during a slowdown, profit margins will get squeezed, and you will have to find ways to lower costs. Knowing higher prices are on the way, though, allows you time to adjust your business strategy.

Unemployment Rate: Measures how many people without jobs are looking for jobs. Rather than focusing on the national or state unemployment rate. Focus on your local unemployment rate because the rates tend to be different from one city or county to the next.

Voting Is Not Enough

Politicians at every level and from both parties enact policies they hope will bring economic prosperity to their districts. Regardless of your political views, your business strategy should mesh with your political environment— but you have to know what your political environment is. This requires you know what your elected officials are doing and what those running for office intend to do.

Stay informed, and monitor economic indicators. They not only impact the world around you, they also impact your bottom line.

Stay informed, and monitor economic indicators.

Chapter 17

Feedback—Good for Business

Before I begin, I want to congratulate you for having the courage to launch your business and the stamina to stay in business. Owning your own business is difficult. Not only are you competing in an ultra-competitive global market, you are also criticized about the way you run your business.

Most of your family and friends who offer their opinions have good intentions, and while it is not easy listening to their criticism, they are only trying to help.

If your family is like mine, they get together during holidays and discuss who is doing what. When I owned my own business and the conversation turned to me, my relatives would pull-up my website and tell me what they thought. Some would visit my website to see if they were interested in buying something, while others would visit to give me their opinions about my website.

I know how it feels being in the hot-seat and getting good-spirited, unsolicited feedback about your business; however, I have to admit that I have also given my share of good-spirited, unsolicited feedback. My family would probably say I have given more than my share.

Comes with the Territory

You have probably discovered that people enjoy telling you what they think about your business—even when you have not asked—and feedback from family and friends is not limited to the holiday season.

Some feedback is mean-spirited and some is tactful, but no matter how it is given, it *is* important. To improve the way your business operates, you need to know what works and what does not; so get in the habit of asking your customers for feedback.

No Obligation

Some business owners do not want feedback—they think it will threaten the way they do business. It does not. Regardless of what anyone says about your business, it is up to you to make the suggested changes. You are not obligated to do so, but if you consider all the feedback offered, you will occasionally find a suggestion that proves helpful.

Accept It

Some people bring things to your attention because they want to help while others do so to highlight your mistakes. Here is how I determine a person's motivation: I ask them

Across the Middle

to write their feedback. If they are willing, they are probably trying to help. If not, they are probably trying to be hurtful. Even if they are trying to be hurtful, I still consider what is said. It is free advice—and it may be good advice.

Website

Your website is your marketing centerpiece, and it will shape more opinions about your business than any single marketing piece. Your website introduces your business to each person who visits, and the first impression is a lasting impression. Friends and relatives may visit your website out of curiosity, but prospective customers will visit for information. Regardless of who visits and why, you need to make a good impression.

If your website touts your business' attention-to-detail, for example, but it has misspelled words on it, then the visitor will conclude your business lacks attention-to-detail. Further, since you have a poorly-written website, they will assume your product or service is also of poor quality.

They will also question your judgment and professionalism because a poorly-written website represents a lack of both. This is not only true for your website: It is true for any marketing piece you circulate.

Not *Just* Your Website

Each marketing piece conveys a message and leaves an impression, so you need a quality copy to leave a good impression. Consider the pieces below, and decide if yours are well-written:

- Advertisements
- Annual Reports
- Biographies
- Blogs
- Brochures
- Case Studies
- Direct Mailers
- Fliers
- LinkedIn Profiles
- (Important) Memorandums
- Newsletter Articles
- Press Releases
- Sales Letters
- Signs
- Testimonials
- Tweets
- White Papers

In addition to getting feedback from family and friends, it is also a good idea to get a professional opinion. If you want feedback about your website or brochure, have an editor or writer review it. Contact mine if you do not know one.

Edward Long is a freelance writer, and he edits my articles. He will be happy to review your marketing pieces. His website is edwardlongkc.com.

Feedback, whether given by a customer in a survey or by a cousin over the phone, is important for your business because no matter how good you are at what you do, you are not an expert at everything. Ask for feedback, use what you can, and dismiss the rest.

Feedback, whether given by a customer in a survey or by a cousin over the phone, is important for your business because no matter how good you are at what you do, you are not an expert at everything.

Chapter 18

Join an Organization

The best way to grow your business is by meeting people and showing them the value of your product or service. You cannot do this too much. If you are uncomfortable networking, do whatever is necessary to overcome your discomfort because networking is vitally important to your business.

Join *at least* one networking organization, which schedules activities for its members to meet, talk, and build business relationships. Some organizations offer additional services: education, training, volunteer work in the community.

There are lots of networking organizations, but the two you should consider first are your local Chamber of Commerce and your industry association (or trade organization).

Chamber of Commerce

Besides organizing networking events, the Chamber of Commerce protects and promotes its local business community by working with business leaders and elected officials to ensure the local business climate is strong.

The Chamber also offers education, training, and volunteer opportunities in the community. Being a Chamber member is also good for business.

A 2012 study, conducted by the Schapiro Group, an Atlanta-based consulting firm, found that 49% of consumers were more likely to think favorably about a local business if it was a member of the local Chamber. It also found that 80% of consumers were more likely to buy a product or service from a business that was a member of the local Chamber.[19]

Industry Association

No matter what product or service you offer, there is an industry association for it—and you should join. An association provides many of the services provided by the Chamber of Commerce with two exceptions.

Unlike the Chamber, your association will keep you abreast of ever-changing issues, trends, and legislation in your industry. In addition, as a member of your association, you can also hold a leadership role.

Do the Work

I have attended networking events all over the country and have noticed there is always at least one person who does one or the other: lays their business cards on the table and walks away or passes their business cards out without talking with the people they have given their cards to.

Neither method is effective. Networking is about building relationships, so you have to take time to ask questions and see if the prospective customer needs what you are offering. Not everyone will. Effective networking requires you to say something memorable so the person knows who you are when you follow-up with a call.

Networking is an art—the more you do it, the better you become. I have watched effective networkers pass-out only ten business cards yet get more business than networkers who passed out 50. Effective networkers build relationships.

Here is a common misconception about being a member of an organization: It will bring business. Organizations do not bring business; they give business owners opportunities to network with other members. To get business, you have to attend the events and build relationships.

First Things First

Before joining an organization, find out who its members are and who it invites to its networking events—big businesses, small businesses—then, based on who you want to meet, decide which organization(s) to join.

If you want to join your local Chamber of Commerce and discover most of its members are business owners, but your ideal customer owns a large business, consider joining a Chamber in a neighboring city that has lots of members who own large businesses.

What Do You Expect?

I have talked to a lot—too many—of business owners who complained they joined an organization, but got nothing out of it. When I asked what they expected to get out of it, they usually said they had no expectations.

That is the problem. No matter how many wonderful activities an organization offers, nor how prestigious membership is, before joining, know exactly what you hope to get from becoming a member.

Joining *at least* one organization should be part of your marketing strategy. The contacts you make, relationships you build, and business you get will more than offset the time and money you have invested. Do not just join, pay your dues, and attend one or two events.

Become an active member and an effective, assertive networker; attend as many events as possible; and seek leadership roles in the organization(s) and in the community.

---

*Become an active
member and an
EFFECTIVE, assertive
NETWORKER; attend as
many events as possible;
and seek LEADERSHIP
roles in the
organization(s) and in the
COMMUNITY.*

Chapter 19

Should the Owner Be Fired?

Corporations and small businesses have a lot in common, which makes sense because a corporation begins as a small business. Both sell a product or service for profit, and both compete for consumers in a crowded market. The biggest difference is not their size: It is that a corporation holds the person at the top accountable for their job performance while a small business typically does not.

Are You Qualified?

A president or CEO is no different from any other corporate employee, and like every other employee, the president or CEO has to go through the application process. They have to be screened and interviewed, and they have to convince human resources they have the experience, skill-set, and temperament to do the job better than the other applicants.

None of these factors apply to business owners. You are not screened or interviewed, you do not need experience in the field in which you are going; and while there is a skill-set you should have, it is not a requirement.

What *Do* You Do?

No matter how large a corporation is, the president or CEO has a job description outlining their duties and responsibilities. It is obvious what they are being paid to do. If you are like most business owners, though, you do not have a job description.

When I meet a business owner for the first time, I ask what they sell, and I ask what they do. Of the hundreds of business owners I have met from across the country, 99% of them said they do everything.

A president or CEO has a well-defined job description, and a business owner should have one too. No matter your title—president, CEO, chairman of the board, senior executive vice president of operations—you should have specific duties and responsibilities because it allows you to spend your time working on them rather than running from crisis to crisis putting-out fires, which is a grossly-inefficient way to run a business.

Do What You Do Best

One of the exercises I teach business owners is how to maximize business' effectiveness and efficiency. I have them list their business' responsibilities, categorize those responsibilities, write job descriptions for each category, and write the name of the employee who handles each responsibility. The resulting organizational chart shows at a glance where the responsibilities lie.

If you are a sole proprietor, you handle all of the responsibilities; but as you hire employees, they assume some of those responsibilities. Your first hires should assume the responsibilities you do not want or that you do not handle well.

If you have been handling marketing, but you are an introvert who gets nervous talking to people, for example, then your first hire should probably be a marketing director. After your business is fully staffed, since the remaining responsibilities are yours to handle, they should be tasks you like and do well.

Are You Good At It?

Having a job description not only lets you know what is expected, it also lets you know how you are performing. A corporation uses evaluations to grade employee performance, including its president or CEO, and it rewards exceptional performance while penalizing poor performance, ensuring each employee performs at a high level.

As a business owner, your performance is not graded. How can it be? If you have no well-defined duties or responsibilities, you have no performance criteria. One of the perks of owning your own business is, you do not have to worry about how well you are doing your job; but for the sake of your business, you *should* be evaluated.

You can establish a board of directors to evaluate your performance, or you can hire an advisory board. An advisory board is separate from your business, and you can meet once a quarter to have them grade your performance. They cannot penalize you for poor performance, but they can let you know if you are doing a good job or not.

Co-Partners

I have met a few business owners in the construction industry who have hired partners to help them run their businesses because they realized this was the most effective and efficient way to run their business.

One of them worked in the office and the other in the field, and whatever their job split—whether 51% to 49% or 60% to 40%—it was far more effective than having one person (i.e., sole proprietor) doing all of the work. These owners saw the value in hiring people with skills they lacked—their businesses were not only successful, they were extraordinarily successful.

Every corporate employee has a job description, has their performance graded annually, and is held accountable for their performance. Why should it be different for a business owner?

A board of directors will dismiss its poorly-performing president or CEO, but do not think a poorly-performing business owner is immune. Small businesses with excellent products or services go out of business every day because the market (i.e., consumers) has no patience for businesses run by inept owners.

Small businesses with EXCELLENT products or services go out of business every day because the MARKET (i.e., consumers) has no PATIENCE for businesses run by inept owners.

Chapter 20

Business is a Race!

In 2014, Dennis Kimetto of Kenya set a world record by running the Berlin Marathon in two hours, two minutes, and fifty-seven seconds. That may sound fast, but if you are a running enthusiast, you know: That is blazing!

The U.S. Army Physical Fitness Guide says, to be in the top 1% of their age group, a seventeen- to twenty-one-year-old runner would have to run one mile in six minutes and thirty seconds, which is a brisk pace. Dennis Kimetto's average mile was four minutes and forty-one seconds, and he sustained that pace for 26.2 miles. Setting a world record.

I discussed speed in a previous chapter (*Don't Move Too Fast*), but I am discussing it again because it is important you understand its importance. While you should not work too fast, most business owners work at a leisurely pace, which indicates they have no idea they are in a race.

An Amazing Race

One of my favorite television programs is *The Amazing Race*. It is exciting, and it is a lot like business. There are teams of two, and the eleven teams complete a series of tasks, which take them around the world. Whichever team completes all of the tasks and reaches the finish line first, wins.

Each day brings a different task, and the team completing that day's task first starts first the next day. If a team completes a task incorrectly, they have to start that task over. Each task must be completed correctly.

To succeed, each team member has to be resourceful and communicate well with their partner, but to succeed in this race—and in business—everyone has to work quickly.

Your Amazing Race

Children do things quickly. When I was young, my parents always told me to slow down. I ran in the house. I ate fast. I needed to slow down then, but when going into business, I realized working quickly was an asset.

You are an adult and a business owner, so I can say this to you: Do not listen to your parents. Or rather, do not heed their calls to slow down. The faster you move in business, the more you get done; and the more sales you make. Resist the temptation to complete every task perfectly. I am not saying to work so fast you produce shoddy work—that will surely put you out of business. Get each task right, of course, but remember: You are in a race.

Pit Stop

Speed is obviously important in auto racing, but a casual viewer may not realize that some of the most important moments in a race occur in the pits. When a driver needs fuel, tires, or an adjustment to their car, they make a pit stop.

The pit crew completes the task quickly and correctly. If the crew does not perform the task quickly, the driver loses valuable seconds; if the crew does not perform the task correctly, the driver could be hurt—or worse—and the car damaged or destroyed.

Each crew performs identical tasks, so the crew performing those tasks the quickest gives their driver an advantage. A one- or two-second advantage gained in the pit can be the difference between winning and finishing second.

Easy Does It

Most business owners approach a task with the intention of completing it perfectly; giving no thought to how long getting it perfect will take. As I said, do everything as well as you can, because quality is of utmost importance; but time is important too.

Assume you are scheduling a meeting with a prospective customer. You have done your homework—studied their product or service, market, and competitors; read their customer reviews; visited their website—and you want to find an interesting fact or anecdote that will make you stand out. To give yourself extra time, you schedule the meeting a day or two later.

As you leave your office on your way to the meeting, you get a call from the prospective customer. They want to cancel. Why? Because they met with one of your competitors the day before and agreed to do business with them.

Running a business is like running a marathon. Trust me—I have done both. It is a *long* way to the finish line, but do not fool yourself by thinking you can jog the race and still win. You cannot. If you run at a leisurely pace, other runners will beat you to the finish line; if you work at a leisurely pace, other business owners will take your share of the market.

Running a business is like running a MARATHON.

Marvin Carolina Jr.

Chapter 21

Where is Your Business Headed?

In his bestseller, *The 7 Habits of Highly Effective People*, Stephen Covey says that highly effective people "start with the end in mind." As a business owner, you should make business decisions based on where you want your business to be in five or ten years. Before making any decision, ask yourself, "Will this get me where I want to go?"

I believe in the power of visualizing and suggest you visualize how you want your business to look in the future. It does not matter how much or how little time you visualize, but do it regularly—and be specific.

Having a goal of making a lot of money is fuzzy; having a goal of $500,000 in annual sales is specific. Your business is yours, and you can make it look any way you want.

To grow your business and realize its potential, you have to consistently make good decisions. I have met too many business owners who have admitted they are in the habit of making decisions that will get them to the next month. Making short-sighted decisions will all-but-ensure you will not arrive where you intended.

Why *are* you in business? If the answer is to make money, then this is not a good reason to be in business. You can make money lots of ways. If providing the best product or service is not your primary reason for being in business, then your competitors—the ones who *are* trying to provide the best product or service—will eventually wrest your market share from you and drive you out of business.

One way to determine where you want your business to go is by working backwards, so start by setting your goal. I cannot overemphasize the importance of goal-setting. Elbert Hubbard, an American philanthropist, said it well; "Many people fail in life, not for lack of ability, or brains or even courage, but simply because they have never organized their energies around a goal."

Highly-effective people set goals. As a business owner, you should not only set goals, you should also communicate them to your employees. Use SMART goals, which means your goals are the following:

Specific: Target a specific area—the more specific the goal, the better.

Measurable: Have tangible criteria for measuring progress.

Assignable: Decide who will do what, and let them know.

Realistic: Decide which results can be achieved, and be willing and able to accomplish the goal given your allotted resources and time.

Time-Sensitive: Specify when it can be achieved. If there is no time limit, there will be no urgency to accomplish the goal.

There are lots of paths you can take in business. With each decision, you either keep your business on the path you want it on or take it down another. Like driving a car, when you leave home, you know where you want to go; so at each intersection, you decide which street will quickly get you to your destination.

A driver can tell you exactly where they want to go and the route they are taking to get there. Make sure you can tell someone the same about your business.

A driver can tell you exactly where they want to go and the ROUTE they are taking to get there. Make sure you can tell someone the same about your business.

End Notes

1. U.S. Small Business Administration, *Small Business Advocate*, September 2012, p. 3.
2. http://www.law360.com/articles/4457/arthur-andersen-to-fight-for-acquital-in-obstruction-case
3. http://www. sleepfoundation.org/sleep-topics/caffeine-and-sleep
4. http://www.ncbi.nlm.nih.gov/pubmed/12683469
5. http://www.forbes.com/sites/melaniehaiken/2014/03/20/lack-of-sleep-kills-brain-cells-new-study-suggests/#3cd88f124986
6. http://www.webmd.com/sleep-disorders/features/how-sleep-affects-your-heart
7. http://www.cdc.gov/features/dssleep
8. U.S. Small Business Administration, *Small Business Advocate*, September 2012, p. 1.
9. http://money.usnews.com/money/blogs/outside-voices-small-business/2009/01/12/why-do-people-become-entrepreneurs
10. http://www.forbes.com/forbes-400/
11. http://money.usnews.com/money/blogs/outside-voices-small-business/2009/01/12/why-do-people-become-entrepreneurs
12. https://www.sageworks.com/blog/post/2013/11/25/Why-businesses-fail-poll.aspx
13. http://www.smallbusinessportal.org/capital
14. https://blogs.microsoft.com/work/2013/10/22/small-business-expert-brian-moran-small-business-owners-are-not-embracing-all-of-the-existing-technology-at-their-disposal/#sm.0001gw4vvow83cobrro26z97t6n6n

15. http://www.forbes.com/sites/erikaandersen/2013/1
    0/07/how-small-business-owners-are-wrecking-their-
    own-chances-of-success/#2f6b6e1b18e7
16. http://www.thesba.com/2013/11/22/how-much-is-
    online-presence-helping-small-business/
17. http://alifeofproductivity.com/why-you-
    procrastinate-10-tactics-to-help-you-stop/
18. http://www.cbsnews.com/news/small-business-
    owners-neglect-retirement-savings/
19. http://www.acce.org/news/2012/11/acce-
    news/survey-chamber-membership-is-effective-
    business-strategy/